CHRISTMAS CAROLS FOR TWO

Arrangements by Mark Phillips

ISBN 978-1-5400-2916-4

HAL•LEONARD®

Contact Us:
Hal Leonard
7777 West Bluemound Road
Milwaukee, WI 53213
Email: info@halleonard.com

In Europe contact:
Hal Leonard Europe Limited
Distribution Centre, Newmarket Road
Bury St Edmunds, Suffolk, IP33 3YB
Email: info@halleonardeurope.com

In Australia contact:
Hal Leonard Australia Pty. Ltd.
4 Lentara Court
Cheltenham, Victoria, 3192 Australia
Email: info@halleonard.com.au

CONTENTS

ANGELS WE HAVE HEARD ON HIGH

CLARINETS

Traditional French Carol

21
25
29
33
36
39

AWAY IN A MANGER

CLARINETS

Music by James R. Murray

17
21
25
29

BRING A TORCH, JEANNETTE, ISABELLA

CLARINETS

17th Century French Provençal Carol

12
16
20
24

DECK THE HALL

CLARINETS

Traditional Welsh Carol

17
21
24
27
30

THE FIRST NOEL

CLARINETS

17th Century English Carol
Music from W. Sandys' *Christmas Carols*

17
21
25
29

GO, TELL IT ON THE MOUNTAIN

CLARINETS

African-American Spiritual

21
25
29
33
37

GOD REST YE MERRY, GENTLEMEN

CLARINETS

Traditional English Carol

Moderately fast

20
24
28
31
35

HARK! THE HERALD ANGELS SING

CLARINETS

Music by Felix Mendelssohn-Bartholdy
Arranged by William H. Cummings

Brightly

21
25
29
33
37

IT CAME UPON THE MIDNIGHT CLEAR

CLARINETS

Music by Richard Storrs Willis

17
21
25
29

JINGLE BELLS

CLARINETS

Words and Music by J. Pierpont

17
21
25
29

JOLLY OLD ST. NICHOLAS

CLARINETS

Traditional 19th Century American Carol

17
21
25
29

JOY TO THE WORLD

CLARINETS

Music by George Frideric Handel
Adapted by Lowell Mason

20
24
28
32
35

O CHRISTMAS TREE

CLARINETS

Traditional German Carol

17
21
25
29

O COME, ALL YE FAITHFUL

CLARINETS

Music by John Francis Wade

21
25
29
33
37

O COME, O COME, EMMANUEL

CLARINETS

15th Century French Melody
Adapted by Thomas Helmore

20
24
27
31
35

O HOLY NIGHT

CLARINETS

Music by Adolphe Adam

26
31
36
41
46

O LITTLE TOWN OF BETHLEHEM

CLARINETS

Music by Lewis H. Redner

17
20
23
26
29

SILENT NIGHT

CLARINETS

Music by Franz X. Gruber

25
29
34
39
44

STILL, STILL, STILL

CLARINETS

Salzburg Melody, c.1819

Moderately slow

13
16
19
22
25

WE THREE KINGS OF ORIENT ARE

CLARINETS

Words and Music by John H. Hopkins, Jr.

17
21
25
29

WE WISH YOU A MERRY CHRISTMAS

CLARINETS

Traditional English Folksong

21
25
29
33
37

WHAT CHILD IS THIS?

CLARINETS

16th Century English Melody

31
37
42
47
53
59

HAL LEONARD PRESENTS

EASY INSTRUMENTAL DUETS

Start your duet playing experience with these fun songbooks! Over 20 easy duet arrangements for two instrumentalists are featured in each of these collections. Woodwind and brass editions can be played together as can the string editions. **Only $9.99 each!**

BROADWAY SONGS FOR TWO

22 showstoppers: Any Dream Will Do • Bring Him Home • Cabaret • Edelweiss • For Forever • Hello, Dolly! • I Believe • Memory • One • Popular • Seasons of Love • Seventy Six Trombones • Tomorrow • Where Is Love? • You've Got a Friend • and more.

00252493 FLUTE
00252494 CLARINET
00252495 ALTO SAX
00252496 TRUMPET
00252497 TROMBONE
00252500 VIOLIN
00252501 CELLO

CLASSICAL THEMES FOR TWO

24 favorite melodies from top classical composers: Air on the G String • Blue Danube Waltz • Canon in D • Eine Kleine Nachtmusik • Hallelujah Chorus • Jesu, Joy of Man's Desiring • Minuet in G Major • Ode to Joy • Pictures at an Exhibition • Sheep May Safely Graze • Trumpet Voluntary • William Tell Overture • and more.

00254439 FLUTE
00254440 CLARINET
00254441 ALTO SAX
00254442 TRUMPET
00254443 TROMBONE
00254444 VIOLIN
00254445 CELLO

CHRISTMAS HITS FOR TWO

22 terrific holiday duets: All I Want for Christmas Is You • Baby, It's Cold Outside • The Christmas Song (Chestnuts Roasting on an Open Fire) • Do You Want to Build a Snowman? • Feliz Navidad • Have Yourself a Merry Little Christmas • It's Beginning to Look like Christmas • Let It Snow! Let It Snow! Let It Snow! • Mary, Did You Know? • Rockin' Around the Christmas Tree • Silver Bells • White Christmas • and more.

00172461 FLUTE
00172462 CLARINET
00172463 ALTO SAX
00172464 TRUMPET
00172465 TROMBONE
00172466 VIOLIN
00172467 CELLO

HIT SONGS FOR TWO

22 mega hits: All About That Bass • All of Me • Brave • Can't Stop the Feeling • Grenade • Hey, Soul Sister • I Will Wait • Let Her Go • 100 Years • Royals • Shake It Off • Shape of You • Stay with Me • Viva La Vida • and more.

00252482 FLUTE
00252483 CLARINET
00252484 ALTO SAX
00252485 TRUMPET
00252486 TROMBONE
00252487 VIOLIN
00252488 CELLO

Prices, contents and availability subject to change without notice.
Sales restrictions to some countries apply.
All prices listed in U.S. funds.

ORDER TODAY FROM YOUR FAVORITE MUSIC RETAILER AT **HALLEONARD.COM**

HAL•LEONARD®

1217